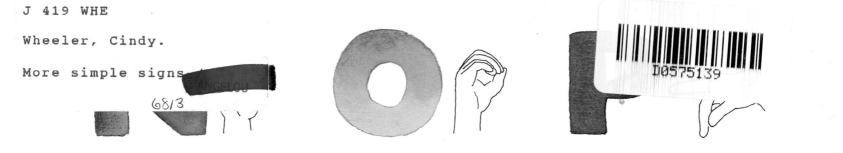

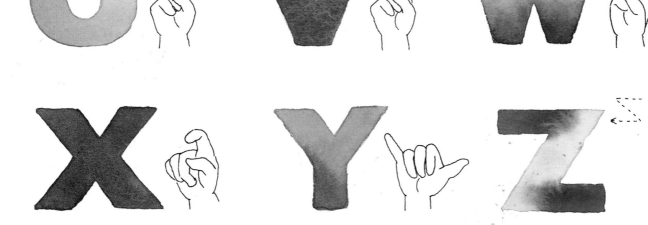

MORE
SIMPLE SIGNS

Cindy Wheeler

VIKING

VIKING
Published by the Penguin Group
Penguin Putnam Inc., 375 Hudson Street, New York, New York 10014, U.S.A.
Penguin Books Ltd, 27 Wrights Lane, London W8 5TZ, England
Penguin Books Australia Ltd, Ringwood, Victoria, Australia
Penguin Books Canada Ltd, 10 Alcorn Avenue, Toronto, Ontario, Canada M4V 3B2
Penguin Books (N.Z.) Ltd, 182-190 Wairau Road, Auckland 10, New Zealand

Penguin Books Ltd, Registered Offices: Harmondsworth, Middlesex, England

First published in 1998 by Viking, a member of Penguin Putnam Inc.

1 3 5 7 9 10 8 6 4 2

LIBRARY OF CONGRESS CATALOGING-IN-PUBLICATION DATA
Wheeler, Cindy.
More simple signs / Cindy Wheeler.
p. cm.
Summary: Teaches twenty-nine signs from American Sign Language
with illustrations and useful hints for remembering them.
ISBN 0-670-87477-9 (hc)
1. American Sign Language—Juvenile literature.
[1. Sign language.] I. Title.
HV2476.W479 419—dc21 1998 97-26797 CIP AC

Manufactured in China
Set in Gill Sans

For Sally —

the best daughter and big sister ever!

sun

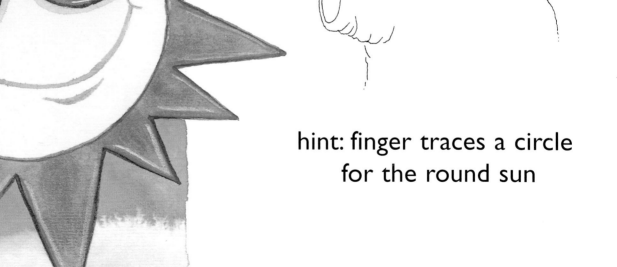

hint: finger traces a circle
for the round sun

hint: hand shows bill of cap

boy

girl

hint: thumb shows
"bonnet strings"

play

hint: make a "y" with your fingers and swing them in a playful motion

jump

hint: make fingers jump in palm of other hand

hint: fingers fold over like legs
sitting in a chair

sit

swing

hint: same sign as sit with added swinging motion

hint: finger presses into cheek
forming a dimple,
like the top of an apple

apple

tree

hint: arm and hand form
tree and twist

hint: fold right pointer finger
down from lips (like red lips)

red

blue

hint: with thumb folded in
on right hand, twist hand
back and forth

yellow

hint: with fingers forming a "y" shape, move hand back and forth and twist wrist

green

hint: right hand makes the letter "g" and shakes slightly back and forth

fish

hint: hand wiggles back and forth like a swimming fish

horse

hint: wiggle two fingers
like a horse's ear

hint: scratch your ribs
like a monkey!

monkey

tiger

hint: show tiger stripes
with fingers

hint: fly fingers of right hand through the air like an airplane

airplane

loud

hint: touch index fingers
to ears, then move hands
out and vibrate
like sound waves

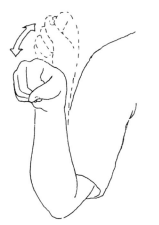

hint: like a head nodding "yes"

yes

no

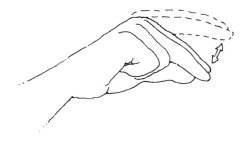

hint: two fingers tap thumb

stop

go

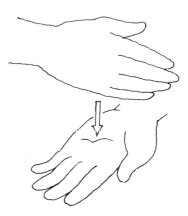

hint: like forming a barrier

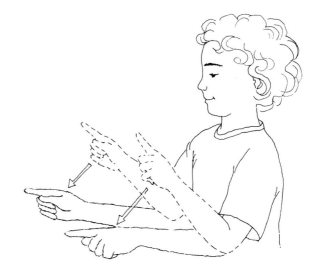

hint: fingers point forward quickly

hint: index fingers jab toward each other and then draw out

hurt

help

hint: one hand lifts
the other fist, like offering
a helping hand

hint: rub heart in circular motion

thank you

hint: like blowing a kiss

hint: draw a house shape
with your hands

house

rain

hint: hands and fingers move like
falling rain drops

hint: like making a rainbow
with your fingertips

rainbow

CINDY WHEELER is the author/
illustrator of many books for chil-
dren, including *Simple Signs, The
Bookstore Cat,* and the popular series
about Marmalade, the striped orange
cat. Ms. Wheeler lives in Asheville,
North Carolina, with her two chil-
dren, Sally and Will.

Jacket illustration copyright © Cindy Wheeler, 1998

VIKING

A Member of Penguin Putnam Inc.

375 Hudson Street

New York, New York 10014

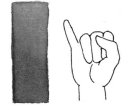